Growing in Love

6

Part of the love story of salvation

PRINCIPAL PROGRAM CONSULTANTS

James J. DeBoy, Jr., MA
Toinette M. Eugene, PhD
Rev. Richard C. Sparks, CSP, PhD

CONSULTANTS

Sr. Jude Fitzpatrick, CHM
Pedagogy

Rev. Mark A. Ressler
Theology

Rev. Douglas O. Wathier
Theology

Daniel J. Bohle, MD (Obstetrics and Gynecology) and Anne Bohle, RN
Family Medicine and Parenting

REVIEWERS

Sr. Connie Carrigan, SSND
Religion Coordinator
Archdiocese of Miami
Miami, Florida

Mark Ciesielski
Associate Director, Office of
Continuing Christian Education
Diocese of Galveston-Houston
Houston, Texas

Margaret Vale DeBoy
Teacher
Arbutus Middle School
Arbutus, Maryland

Diane Dougherty
Director of Children's and
Family Catechesis
Archdiocese of Atlanta
Atlanta, Georgia

Harry J. Dudley, D. Min.
Associate Executive Director
of Faith Formation
Archdiocese of Indianapolis
Indianapolis, Indiana

Steven M. Ellair
Diocesan Consultant for
Elementary Catechesis
Archdiocese of Los Angeles
Los Angeles, California

Kirk Gaddy
Principal
St. Katharine Campus/
Queen of Peace School
Baltimore, Maryland

Connie McGhee
Principal
Most Holy Trinity School
San Jose, California

Barbara Minczewski
Religion Formation
Coordinator
Diocese of Davenport
Davenport, Iowa

Sr. Judy O'Brien, IHM
Rockville Centre, New York

Kenneth E. Ortega
Consultant for Media and
Curriculum
Diocese of Joliet
Joliet, Illinois

Sr. Barbara Scully, SUSC
Assistant Director of Religious
Education
Archdiocese of Boston
Randolph, Massachusetts

Rev. John H. West, STD
Theological Consultant,
Department of Education
Archdiocese of Detroit
Rector, St. John's Center for
Youth and Families
Plymouth, Michigan

Our Sunday Visitor

Curriculum Division

Nihil Obstat
Rev. Richard L. Schaefer
Censor Deputatus

Imprimatur
✠ Most Rev. Jerome Hanus, OSB
Archbishop of Dubuque
January 28, 2000
Feast of Saint Thomas Aquinas, Patron of Chastity and of Students

The Ad Hoc Committee to Oversee the Use of the Catechism, National Conference of Catholic Bishops, has found this catechetical text, copyright 2001, to be in conformity with the *Catechism of the Catholic Church.*

The nihil obstat and imprimatur are official declarations that a book or pamphlet is free of doctrinal or moral error. No implication is contained herein that those who granted the nihil obstat and imprimatur agree with the contents, opinions, or statements expressed.

Photography Credits
AP/Wide World Photos: 57; Bob Daugherty: 33; **Art Resource, NY:** Giraudon: 13; **Comstock:** 7, 46; **Gene Plaisted/ The Crosiers:** 12, 19, 21, 36, 43, 49; **Digital Imaging Group:** 8, 9, 14, 15, 24, 49, 52, 56, 59; **Susie Fitzhugh:** 40; **FPG International:** Josef Beck: 29; Montes De Oca: 46; Paul Markow: 4, 11; Telegraph Colour Library: 6; **Jack Holtel:** 15, 16, 22, 28, 30, 32, 35, 36, 40, 41, 45, 57; **The Image Bank:** David W. Hamilton: 46; **Stephen G. Maka:** 39; **Natural Bridges:** Robert Lentz: 55; **PhotoDisc, Inc.:** Jack Hollingsworth: 21; **Stock Boston:** Eastcott/Momatiuk: 46; Robert Fried: 48; **The Stock Market:** Nancy Ney: 7; **Tony Stone Images:** Barbara Filet: 44, 51; ESA/K. Horgan: 4; Ken Fisher: 54; Robert Kusel: 6; David Madison: 7, 12; Michael Townsend: 28; **Superstock:** 20, 27, 45; **Unicorn Stock Photos:** Jean Higgins: 23; Ron Holt: 25

Cover
Photo by **Jack Holtel**
Illustration by **Francis Livingston**

ISBN: 978-0-15-950668-4
Item Number: CU2103

7 8 9 10 11 015016 15 14 13 12 11 10
Manufactured by Webcrafters, Inc., Madison WI,
United States of America, August 2010, Job #87513

Growing
in
Love

6

God our Father, your love overflowed into creation and gave us the gift of life. Jesus, help us choose life and all that is good. Holy Spirit, make us aware of our holiness and worth. Amen.

Life from Love

Imagine getting the greatest gift ever. What would it be? How would you show that you liked it?

Now picture the world at its best, filled with people, animals, trees, and plants. It's all yours! You've already been given a great gift by the most generous giver: God gave you all of creation, especially living creatures.

Whew! How does a person say thanks for such an incredible gift? Think about gifts you've received from people. Some of them you didn't like, and maybe you put them under the bed or in the closet. Others may have been so special that you handled them with care. The gift of creation is an expression of God's great love for you. It's meant to be used and enjoyed with appreciation and respect.

In God's wisdom all creation is interconnected. The bee and the buzzard, the redwood and the rose, people and pets—all living things have an interdependent relationship. They need one another to survive. When you care for creation, in a sense you care for yourself. You are a chord in the harmony of creation.

When we see how beautiful yet how fragile our planet looks from space, we understand the importance of treating the earth and each other more respectfully.

Although we are connected to all living things, humans are unique. As the Book of Genesis tells us, God breathed life into humans. *(See Genesis 2:7.)* We have been made in God's image and likeness, as male or female, to live in relationship with God and with one another.

Of all the life that has been created, only people have the privilege of consciously knowing, loving, and serving God. We express our love for God in the way we treat all living things. In fact, as we relate to each other and to our world in ways that are life-giving, we become co-creators with God.

Life Is Sacred

Catholics
Believe

God alone is the
Lord of life from
life's beginning
until its end.

*(See Catechism,
#2258.)*

Have you ever noticed how some people are
ignored by others or are laughed at, even when
nothing is funny? If you've ever been the one
who is ignored or laughed at, you know how
much that can hurt.

Church teachings on life are based on Jesus'
example and teachings. Jesus respected each
person as a child of God and excluded no one.
He showed us that every life is to be honored as
sacred, or holy, at every stage.

As Christians we know that we don't own our
bodies. They are gifts from God. God wants us to
treasure and nurture life in ourselves and in
creation. Any action that deliberately destroys
God's sacred gift of life, such as **abortion**, is sinful.

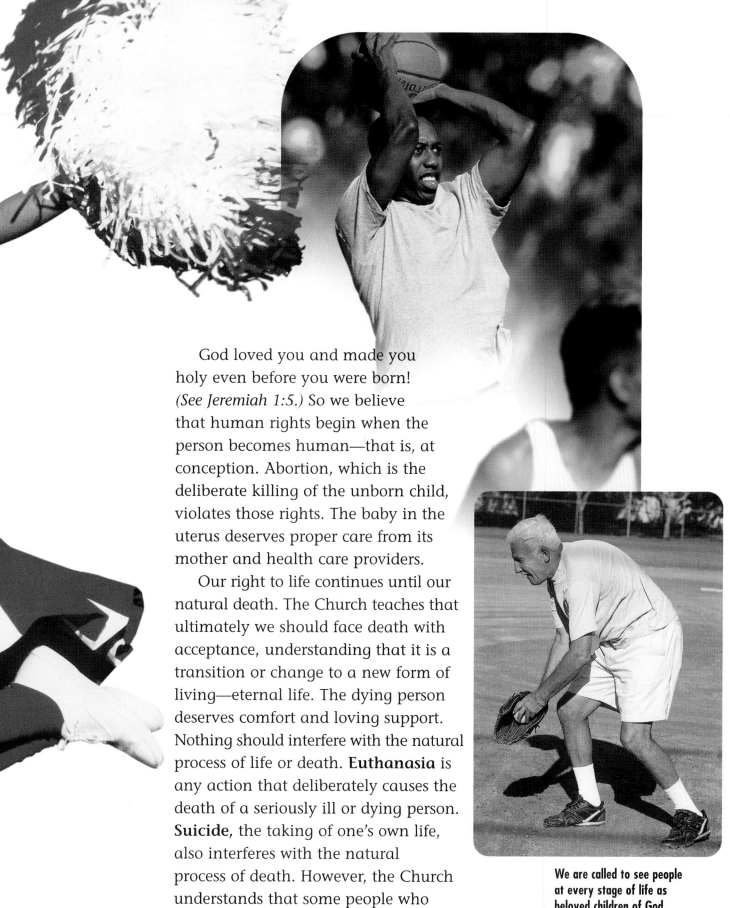

God loved you and made you holy even before you were born! *(See Jeremiah 1:5.)* So we believe that human rights begin when the person becomes human—that is, at conception. Abortion, which is the deliberate killing of the unborn child, violates those rights. The baby in the uterus deserves proper care from its mother and health care providers.

Our right to life continues until our natural death. The Church teaches that ultimately we should face death with acceptance, understanding that it is a transition or change to a new form of living—eternal life. The dying person deserves comfort and loving support. Nothing should interfere with the natural process of life or death. **Euthanasia** is any action that deliberately causes the death of a seriously ill or dying person. **Suicide,** the taking of one's own life, also interferes with the natural process of death. However, the Church understands that some people who are overwhelmed by serious problems may not be fully responsible for their decision to take their own lives.

We are called to see people at every stage of life as beloved children of God.

Choosing Life

Why do I have to shower?
Why do I have to do homework?
Why do I need to go to church?
Surprisingly, these questions can all have the same
answer: Doing this shows **self-respect.**

Respecting yourself means cherishing the gift
of life God has given you. You do this by practicing
temperance—making moderate, healthy choices that
show you care about your physical, mental, emotional,
and spiritual health.

Physical Health

Your body is going through an intense growth spurt,
and habits you form now will affect your whole life.
So it's good to focus on healthy habits, such as eating
nutritionally, exercising regularly, and keeping clean.
You can decide now to avoid dangerous, life-threatening
habits involving drugs, tobacco products,
and alcohol.

**You'll find many opportunities to use
your God-given intelligence to explore
the wonders of creation.**

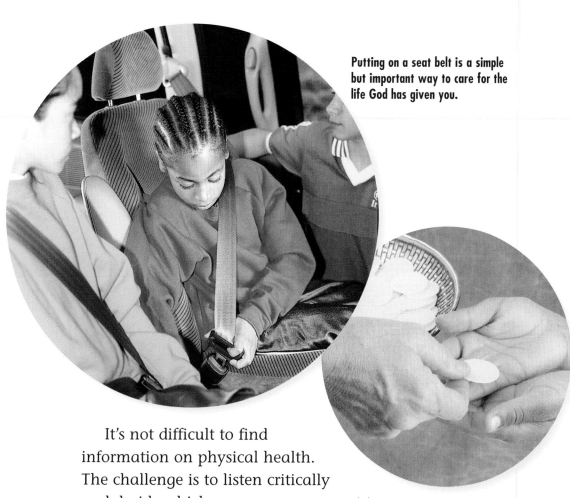

Putting on a seat belt is a simple but important way to care for the life God has given you.

The Eucharist is a source of spiritual strength and health for you now and throughout your life.

It's not difficult to find information on physical health. The challenge is to listen critically and decide which messages are meant to help you and which are meant to sell certain products.

Mental and Emotional Health

Having a curious mind and an eagerness to learn new things keeps your brain cells developing and promotes a longer life. What we learn helps us and helps our world be better. When your emotions seem to be out of control, like a roller coaster, try to name one specific emotion you're feeling. Then identify the source of the emotion, particularly if you're feeling angry, fearful, or sad. Finally, use the emotion to help you learn something about yourself or to move yourself to do the right thing.

Spiritual Health

You are much more than your physical, mental, and emotional self. Your spirit helps define who you are. You care for your spirit by accepting yourself with all your strengths and weaknesses. Find out more about yourself by staying close to God through prayer and the sacraments. Write some of your thoughts in a journal. Pursue interests and activities that help you be the best person possible.

Scripture Signpost

I have set before you life and death, the blessing and the curse. Choose life, then, that you and your descendants may live.

(Deuteronomy 30:19)

Life Is Good

Think about the stages of life pictured on pages 6 and 7, and then make a magazine ad that encourages respect for life. Draw a picture or glue a photo of someone in one of those stages. Add a message to persuade a reader to show respect for life at that stage.

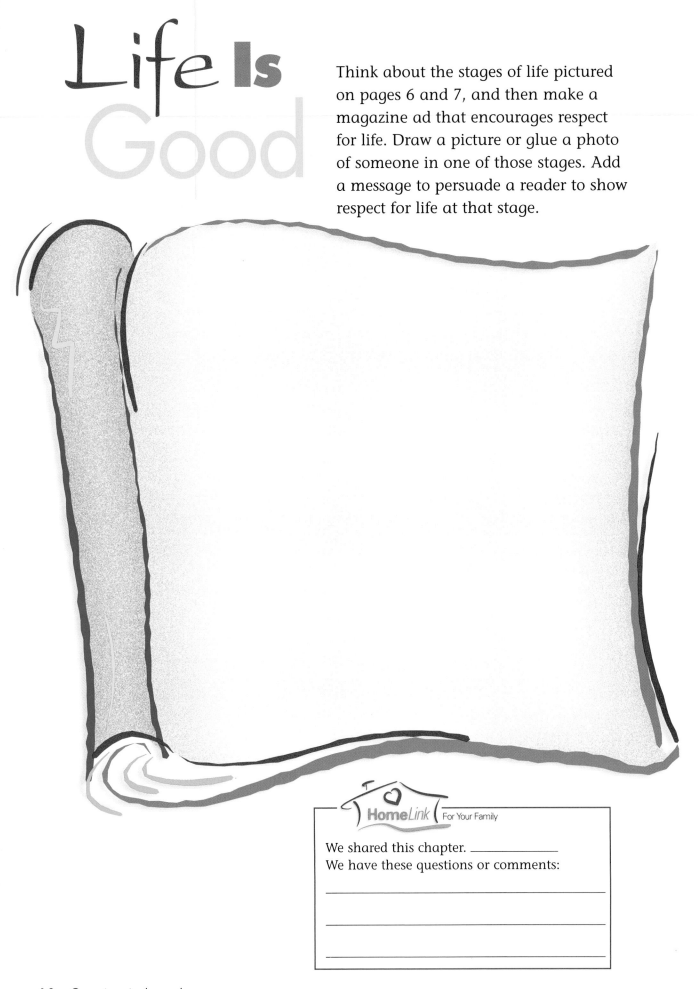

HomeLink For Your Family

We shared this chapter. _____
We have these questions or comments:

_____

_____

_____

The glory of **God** is a **person** fully alive.

(Saint Irenaeus)

Chapter 2

God our Father, you call us to join you in a trusting, covenant relationship. Jesus Christ, show us how to respond to this call. Holy Spirit, fill us with love for God, others, and ourselves. Amen.

Covenant of Love

Most agreements that we make are based on trust. We may send a check to a publisher and expect a monthly magazine in exchange. Or we form friendships and expect loyalty in return.

Not all of life is this dramatic or challenging, but our relationships with God and with others all depend on trust.

Some agreements are more serious than others because they form the basis for our ongoing relationships, such as the lifelong bond that a husband and wife develop over the years.

Throughout history people have tried to work things out by making very serious, specific promises called **covenants.** Covenants have joined the parties in permanent, personal relationships. Any person or group who broke a covenant could expect certain specific consequences.

Throughout salvation history God has constantly reminded his people how to live their covenant relationship with him and with one another. God calls each of us to join with him in an everlasting, close relationship—a covenant relationship that is based on trust and sealed in love.

At this time in your life, part of your covenant with God is being the best person you can be. Keeping this covenant involves developing good relationships based on trust and loyalty. Such relationships can help prepare you for future covenant relationships such as marriage, the priesthood, or religious life.

The Jesse tree, a traditional way of showing our ancestors in faith, expresses the covenant in the form of a family tree.

Love God, Love Others

Catholics Believe

The Great Commandment is the twofold yet single commandment of love.

(See Catechism, #2055.)

God the Father sent Jesus to fulfill the covenant with his people. Through Jesus, God promises us everlasting life and love; in return, we promise to love God, ourselves, and others. Jesus summed up our duties toward God and others in the Great Commandment: "You shall love the Lord, your God, with all your heart, with all your being, with all your strength, and with all your mind, and your neighbor as yourself" *(Luke 10:27).*

The Great Commandment speaks first of love of God because the everyday choices and decisions we make are based on this love.

Our love of God can lead us to simple acts of charity, such as preparing food for those who are hungry.

As Christians we live the virtue of justice by giving people what they deserve as children of God.

Loving God leads to loving ourselves and others. Usually we love people because they love us. This isn't hard to do. But God calls us to a deeper love that is so unselfish that it doesn't expect anything in return; we are called to love others because God has loved us and because we love God. The virtue of Christian **charity**, or love, requires action—looking around and seeing who needs your time, your smile, your friendship, your conversation, your attention, or even your possessions.

Loving others also involves a sense of **justice**, which is a true and genuine fairness. Fairness is usually thought of as playing by the rules. Justice, however, tries to establish rules where there don't seem to be any or to replace unjust rules with better ones. Christian justice stems from our covenant with God. It is a virtue driven by the belief that all people should receive what they are due because they are children of God. *(See 1 John 3:16–18.)* This belief goes hand in hand with action: it leads us to make deliberate choices to get out there and do something for those who are in need.

Stepping Stones

Building Self-Esteem

Loving and accepting yourself is a first step toward loving and accepting others. Here are some tips:

- **Think about your strengths and gifts every day. Thank God for them.**

- **Accept the ups and downs of life. With your family, figure out ways to handle stress and challenges.**

- **Know that it's okay to feel discouraged and to make mistakes. Some of your choices may lead to bad actions, but you still have the dignity of a person loved by God.**

- **Choose supportive friends who try to make good choices.**

- **Learn to express your feelings with honesty.**

- **Say no to anything self-destructive so that you are in charge of your life.**

God Calls

Prayer—talking and listening to God—is a way to say *yes* to a close friendship with God. God calls each of us to be closely connected to him in a covenant relationship.

You may know some people who talk to you only when they want something. If you have that kind of communication with God, what does that say about your relationship with him? Being in a loving relationship with God involves more than asking for things now and then. You need to pray daily and talk with God about everyday things that are important to you.

Some people confuse praying with wishing. They step up to the free throw line and ask God for help in making the basket. You can pray to do your best, but God hasn't promised to be your personal magician. Pray with the belief that God is always there for you and loves you, and trust that he will guide you in doing what is right.

Because our relationships with other people are an important part of our lives, we need to include our concerns for others and our feelings for them in our prayers also. Always remember that prayer is a place of meeting, a keeping in touch—a place of covenant.

—We Respond

Think of a time when you felt very closely connected to a friend. Maybe you were talking, laughing, or just hanging out together. People who become friends figure out ways to keep the friendship strong. They come to see the importance of frequent, honest communication.

Good communication involves both talking and listening. Thinking about what you're going to say next, instead of really listening, can bring communication to a halt. Sometimes what should be a dialogue turns into two monologues. A true listener, however, hears the other person with both head and heart and responds with respect.

The words we use in our communication with others can affirm them or put them down. The better we feel about ourselves, the more likely we are to use affirming language with others. When we compliment and praise people for their qualities or accomplishments, we are affirming them. If we call people names or make them feel bad about themselves, we are missing an opportunity to communicate well and we are damaging our friendships. Good communication deepens our relationships.

Witness Words

Prayer enlarges the heart until it is capable of containing God's gift of himself.

(Mother Teresa)

Love Builds

On each brick of the bottom layer, name an act of love or justice that you notice at your school. On each brick above the foundation, describe a loving or just action that you would like to see.

HomeLink For Your Family

We shared this chapter. _____
We have these questions or comments:

_____

_____

_____

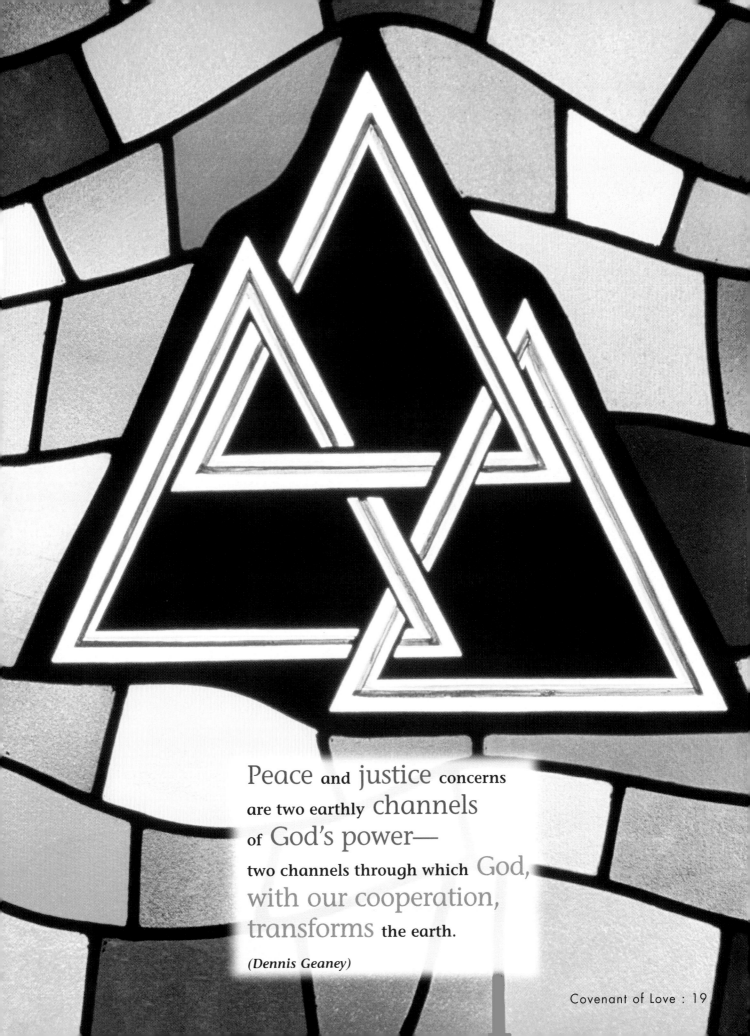

Peace and justice concerns are two earthly channels of God's power— two channels through which God, with our cooperation, transforms the earth.

(Dennis Geaney)

Chapter 3

God our Father, thank you for calling us to love others. Jesus, Son of God, open our eyes so we may see what they need from us. Holy Spirit, move us to act with compassion and sacrifice. Amen.

Christian Love

Christianity is centered in the Paschal mystery, or the amazing truth that Jesus willingly lived, died, and was raised from death for us. Why did Jesus live among us and give up his life? You say the answer at Mass: "Dying you destroyed our death; rising you restored our life." Jesus died to save us from the power of sin and everlasting death so that we can have new life with God now and forever.

Jesus of Nazareth often helped a particular person die to his or her old self and give birth to a new self. When those who sinned were forgiven, they gave up their wrongful ways and became Jesus' disciples.

We share in Christ's Paschal mystery in the sacraments of the Church. Our celebration of the sacraments shows our willingness to leave behind a sinful way of living in order to live in the fullness of God's kingdom. This life journey begins with Baptism, the sacrament of rebirth. Each day we try to live the commitment made at Baptism to love God, ourselves, and others.

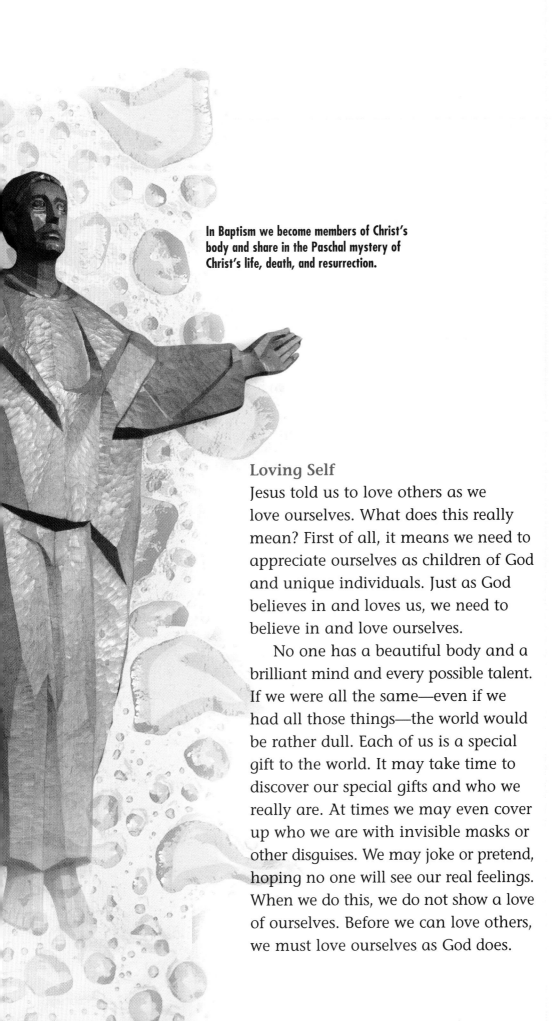

In Baptism we become members of Christ's body and share in the Paschal mystery of Christ's life, death, and resurrection.

Loving Self

Jesus told us to love others as we love ourselves. What does this really mean? First of all, it means we need to appreciate ourselves as children of God and unique individuals. Just as God believes in and loves us, we need to believe in and love ourselves.

No one has a beautiful body and a brilliant mind and every possible talent. If we were all the same—even if we had all those things—the world would be rather dull. Each of us is a special gift to the world. It may take time to discover our special gifts and who we really are. At times we may even cover up who we are with invisible masks or other disguises. We may joke or pretend, hoping no one will see our real feelings. When we do this, we do not show a love of ourselves. Before we can love others, we must love ourselves as God does.

Understanding and Loving

When we pay attention to the needs and feelings of others, we begin to see ways that we can share God's love with them.

When you were little, did you ever try tramping along in an adult's big shoes? Did you ever slip your feet into high heels? For those few faltering steps, you felt all grown up.

You're older now, and yet you're at just the right age to put on other people's shoes. The Native American saying, "To know a man, walk a mile in his moccasins," is good advice for following the Great Commandment. You may be ready to walk in other people's shoes again, this time not to pretend that you're grown up but to learn more about how other people feel. Getting into another's shoes is a way to see that person without prejudice or judgment. It can help you see all people as God's chosen ones, who deserve your respect.

Loving Others

Some shoes may have stomped away from you in anger. Their wearers may have caused you pain or hurt your feelings. Put on those shoes, and think about what may have prompted the outburst. Understanding leads to forgiveness.

Even when we're not sure what needs to be done, we can take time to be with those who are hurting.

Notice the shoes that people wear. Maybe they don't carry a brand name or aren't in style. They could be specially constructed orthopedic shoes, or they could be thick and sturdy shoes to support aging feet. Step inside these shoes, and come to know that people are far more than what they own or what they wear; they are more than any of the things that limit them. Understanding leads to kindness.

There are people wearing shoes that are so worn, the soles are padded with torn cardboard. There are feet covered by soiled shoes found in a trash bin or second-hand shoes given at a shelter. Slip inside these shoes, and imagine the pain and possible shame of the wearer. Think of reasons the person can't buy a new pair of shoes. Understanding leads to **compassion**, a genuine care for someone who is suffering.

Most people you see are wearing ordinary shoes in everyday experiences. Some shoes may drag along the floor because their wearer is sad, lonely, or fearful. Other shoes tap or dash or dance, giving hints of happier feelings. Slip on the shoes of the people around you. Be patient and attentive to their sorrows and sincerely interested in their well-being. Understanding leads to care.

What makes such caring actions signs of Christian love? It's the motivation. "Let us love one another, because love is of God" *(1 John 4:7)*.

Scripture
Signpost

Put on then, as God's chosen ones, holy and beloved, heartfelt compassion, kindness, humility, gentleness, and patience. And over all these put on love.
(Colossians 3:12, 14)

A Caring Framework

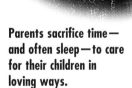

Parents sacrifice time—and often sleep—to care for their children in loving ways.

At the Last Supper, after telling his apostles about the challenges of love, Jesus said, "No one has greater love than this, to lay down one's life for one's friends" *(John 15:13)*. His was the ultimate sacrifice. Most of us will not have to prove our love by giving up our lives. However, Jesus' words also teach us that we need to ask, "What can I do that is for the good of the other person?"

All relationships are built on mutual support. Two qualities that help form the framework of support are self-sacrifice and discipline. These qualities help us put the needs of all in perspective. You can practice self-sacrifice and discipline in the relationships you have now with your family, friends, Church, and teams or other groups, and in the relationships you form as you grow into adulthood.

Self-sacrifice literally means giving of one's self. But self-sacrifice can also be thought of as a gift of something else—time, help, or money—for another person's happiness or well-being. For example, the adult members of the family may sacrifice by saving money to provide a good education for the children.

Discipline is not punishment. Rather it helps put you, not your impulses, in charge of your life. Discipline requires you to make some choices about what's important and helps you develop greater care for yourself and for others. It takes discipline to listen to another person's point of view and to eat and play in moderation.

It also takes discipline to say no to what is bad or inappropriate in a relationship. This is especially true in the area of sexuality. Attraction to a person of the other gender and other sexual feelings can be very strong during the teen years. To act on these feelings is inappropriate because young people are not ready for the commitment of marriage. Our conscience helps us judge whether an action on our part is right or wrong, and discipline helps us carry through on the right decision.

Sometimes a young person becomes a victim of **sexual abuse** without understanding what is happening. An adult who eventually sexually abuses a child may begin with caring actions, thus gaining the child's confidence. The child has no way of knowing whether that adult may sexually abuse him or her. An adult who sexually abuses a child is doing something that is both criminally and morally wrong. The victim is not at fault. Relationships that are verbally or physically abusive are also wrong. A young person involved in any of these abusive or otherwise inappropriate relationships ought to talk to a trusted adult at once. It takes discipline and strength to take a stand against noncaring relationships.

Growing relationships depend on a caring framework woven by discipline and self-sacrifice, much like this carefully constructed nest.

The Good Samaritan

Retold by _____

In the Bible story a man who's been robbed and beaten needs help, but he is ignored by two people who are usually thought of as caring. An unlikely person shows the victim compassion. Write a modern-day version of the story.

AN UNLIKELY HERO

_____

_____

_____

_____

_____

_____

HomeLink For Your Family

We shared this chapter. _____

We have these questions or comments:

_____

_____

_____

For I am convinced that neither death, nor life, nor angels, nor principalities, nor present things, nor future things, nor powers, nor height, nor depth, nor any other creature will be able to separate us from the love of God in Christ Jesus our Lord.

(Romans 8:38–39)

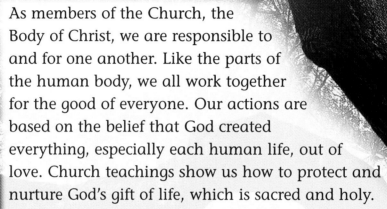

Chapter 4

God our Father, you bless us with others to love. Jesus, show us how to bring your love into our relationships with our family and friends. Holy Spirit, give us a sense of responsibility to care for those who need us. Amen.

Practicing Love?

As members of the Church, the Body of Christ, we are responsible to and for one another. Like the parts of the human body, we all work together for the good of everyone. Our actions are based on the belief that God created everything, especially each human life, out of love. Church teachings show us how to protect and nurture God's gift of life, which is sacred and holy.

The Church's teachings, which are based on Jesus' teachings, have stood the test of time. They show us good ways to live. These teachings come to us through the **magisterium,** or teaching authority, of the Church. Through the power of the Holy Spirit, the bishops in union with the pope lead us and show us how to be faithful to these teachings, as well as to our families and communities.

Church teachings can be applied to all areas where people are called to make decisions. These teachings are especially important today in decisions involving **bioethics,** where people are struggling with issues related to health care and research on human life.

This tree has strong roots that help keep it healthy. How do Church teachings and the natural moral law help us live a healthy life?

We are created as sexual beings, and Church teachings help us value our sexuality and live responsibly.

Human life and sexuality issues raise questions that call for the right use of God's gift of life. Church teachings on who we are as sexual beings in today's world are sometimes quite different from what is seen in the media. The underlying principles of the teachings emphasize the positive and the good: Each person has the right to be treated with dignity. All life is sacred, holy, and blessed by God.

Church teachings have strong roots in the **natural moral law**, the God-given moral sense that helps us tell right from wrong. It is called *natural* because it is found within human nature. It's called *moral* because it is related to right behavior. It's a *law* because it governs people's conduct. All people have a sense of the natural moral law, though different individuals or cultures may express it in different terms.

The Fabric of Love

The Church has the right and duty to announce moral principles.

(See Catechism, #2032.)

The teachings of the Church are interwoven like a seamless garment. One belief connects to another, creating a body of teachings that show God's love for us as it has been revealed by Jesus, the Son, and inspired by the Spirit.

Like strands of yarn woven closely together, the teachings are strong and durable. Like a repeated pattern, the teachings are consistent; they do not change to reflect the fads or trends of a particular time. An action that is wrong is always wrong, no matter how you feel when you are doing it. Like fabric that is the same, yard after yard, the teachings are consistent. Through its teachings the Church applies the natural moral law and the gospel to new situations and issues. For example, in recent years Church leaders have applied these teachings as they have evaluated the morality of cloning.

Teachings on Sexuality

The Church teaches that sexuality is an awesome gift and responsibility. Sexuality affects the total person, especially his or her relationships and the ability to procreate. God blesses the union of man and woman which we call marriage. The Catholic Church celebrates the marriage of two baptized persons as a sacrament. The wife and husband make sacred promises of a lifelong commitment to fidelity. These vows make their marriage more than an ordinary agreement. It is a covenant relationship.

An act of adultery—sexual relations between two persons, at least one of whom is married to another—breaks the vow of faithfulness. It is morally wrong because it shows great disrespect for the holiness of the marriage union, for the married partner, for oneself, and for the covenant. Adultery is one reason some couples divorce. Divorce goes against the teachings of Jesus and the deep-seated desire in humans for marital fidelity and family stability. Divorce has long-range negative effects on both partners, especially if one of them is blameless; on their children; and on society.

Unmarried persons, no matter what their vocation or sexual orientation, are to practice **abstinence** and refrain from sexual intercourse. Outside of marriage this intimate act fails to reflect the unitive and procreative dimensions of sexual intercourse, which require the total commitment of the couple.

Sexual abuse is the mistreatment of another person through improper sexual contact. Rape and incest are the two most common forms of sexual abuse. A person who sexually abuses another commits a crime and a grave moral wrong. The victim is not responsible for the action of the abuser nor guilty of any sin. All forms of abuse—physical, emotional, and sexual—damage relationships, and they are always wrong. Anyone who becomes aware of an abusive situation has an obligation to report the crime to the proper authorities so the abuse can be stopped and the victim helped.

Reaching Out

Many parishes and church-related organizations serve people who are lonely, unloved, or excluded from the larger society.

As members of the Church, our challenge is to love the unloved—people who suffer from loneliness, sin, pain, exclusion, abuse, or illness, and even people who have caused others to suffer. Our response to these people is based on the example and teachings of Jesus.

What Jesus Teaches

At the sight of the crowds, his heart was moved with pity for them because they were troubled and abandoned . . . (Matthew 9:36).

We are called as individuals and as a Church to be compassionate, as Jesus was. This often means working for social justice and doing works of charity. Church organizations all over the world give hope to those who feel abandoned. Casa Juan Diego in Houston serves immigrants and refugees and tries to meet their immediate needs. It offers shelter, English classes, food, medicine, and clothing. Saint Anne's home in Los Angeles offers a safe place to pregnant teens, many of whom have been abused. While living at Saint Anne's, these young women receive medical care, learn parenting skills, and continue their education.

Babies with AIDS are children of God who need special care to enable them to be as healthy as they can be.

And then a leper approached, did him homage, and said, "Lord, if you wish, you can make me clean." He stretched out his hand, touched him, and said, "I will do it" (Matthew 8:2–3).

As Jesus cared for those whom others shunned, so does the Church. This is particularly evident in the way it reaches out to those infected with **HIV** and those suffering from **AIDS.** The bishops have set directives for serving those suffering from AIDS-associated illnesses and for their caregivers. Places like the Catholic AIDS Ministry in Seattle provide a welcoming environment where people who are HIV-positive and their loved ones may gather and feel supported.

"Whatever you did for one of these least brothers of mine, you did for me" (Matthew 25:40).

The bishops in the United States have directed parishes to promote social justice in their schools and religious education programs by teaching about and working for the basic rights all people are due. Many parishes and diocesan groups have justice and peace programs to help their members feed people who are hungry, clothe those who are poor, aid those who are helpless, visit those in prison, give shelter to those who are homeless, and offer assistance to women with unwanted pregnancies and compassion to women who suffer the aftereffects of abortions.

Witness Words

Everyone has an obligation to be at the service of life. This responsibility requires concerted and generous action by all the members of the Christian community.

(Pope John Paul II, "The Gospel of Life")

The Courage to Love

People who are ill are often helped by the healing actions of doctors and nurses. When we are afraid to reach out to others, we may need some healing, too. Be the doctor or nurse for a few minutes, and suggest a healing action to help a person overcome his or her fear of reaching out. Suggest what the person could read, learn, pray about, or do to find the courage to reach out.

Patient's Chart

Condition: Fear of being a friend to someone with AIDS

Healing action suggested:

_____

_____

_____

_____

_____

Signature: _____

Patient's Chart

Condition: Fear of talking to someone who is ignored or laughed at

Healing action suggested:

_____

_____

_____

_____

_____

Signature: _____

HomeLink For Your Family

We shared this chapter. _____
We have these questions or comments:

_____

_____

The joy and hope, the grief and anguish of the people of our time, especially of those who are poor or afflicted in any way, are the joy and hope, grief and anguish of the followers of Christ as well. Nothing that is genuinely human fails to find an echo in our hearts.

(Vatican II, "Pastoral Constitution on the Church in the Modern World")

Chapter 5

God our Father, you give us the grace to be whole and holy in all that we do. Jesus, show us how to face the temptations that we meet in our relationships. Holy Spirit, guide us to choose friends who bring out the best in us. Amen.

Holy and Whole

To My Child Love, God

A phrase in Colossians 3:12 reads, "God's chosen ones, holy and beloved." That describes you! God gives you **grace**, the loving gift of himself, which makes you holy. Grace is also God's help in responding to the call to holiness. God freely gives you grace, out of love for you. Think of grace as your friendship with God. The closeness of your relationship depends on how much you allow God's life to work in you.

God Calls Us

No matter what vocation we have, all of us are called by God to live a life of love—loving and respecting God, our neighbor, and ourselves. We respond to this call when we accept ourselves and others as God made us, with all our strengths and weaknesses. God's loving relationship with us makes us whole.

When we are open to God's love for us, we can give our full commitment to a life of love. It's quite a challenge to live this way. This commitment calls us to see ourselves and others as God sees us, whole and holy, and to respect ourselves and others. God's grace helps us look beyond what we may feel like doing right now and make decisions based on what is right and what is best for everyone.

We grow in relationship with God as we share in his life through the sacraments. In the Eucharist we become one with Jesus, whose life, death, and resurrection show the fullness of God's love for us. We also come to know God's love for us through creation, Scripture, our experiences, and the love of others, and particularly through the life of Jesus. Reconciliation offers us God's forgiveness, which in turn gives us the courage to forgive others.

Grace comes to us through the power of the Holy Spirit, and praying to the Spirit helps us keep our relationship with God strong. Grace is a gift that keeps on giving. The more we live in God's way, the closer we come to God. The closer we come to God, the more we live in God's way.

Attractions and Temptations

We were created in God's image and likeness to share in his goodness and love. Sin, a deliberate turning away from God, is also a turning away from good. Because of original sin we have a tendency to choose what is wrong. This tendency is called **concupiscence.** Because of concupiscence, sin is attractive. Throughout our lives we will be tempted to sin, to do what is harmful to ourselves and others.

Picture some things you have that you really like, and think about what you do to take care of them. Now imagine the kind of care the most important people in your life deserve. People—yourself included—are what give your life value. Most of life is spent with others, so it's natural that temptations occur within relationships. You probably have several relationships—with family members, friends, classmates, teammates—and have figured out suitable ways to behave in each relationship. As you develop your relationships with persons of the other gender, you will need to rely on chastity to help you treat each person with respect. Sins against chastity are ways we misuse God's gift of sexuality.

Lust is an excessive desire for sexual pleasure only, with little or no concern for intimacy and without commitment or responsibility toward the other person. When we let our lustful feelings rule us, the other person becomes for us an object and not a full person. And we degrade ourselves and our own wholeness and holiness.

Masturbation is the deliberate self-stimulation of the genitals solely for one's own sexual pleasure. It is an abuse of sexuality because it does not fulfill the God-given purpose of sexual activity; that is, it does not promote the loving unity of a couple and it does not contribute to procreation.

Sexual intercourse outside of marriage reduces the unifying act of love expressed by married couples to something less than God intended. Sexual activity outside of marriage is not based in lifelong commitment, and it often involves deceiving another person. Teenagers who become involved in sexual relationships are often looking for love and acceptance but find instead that they have been used. The Church believes that the lifelong commitment of marriage promotes good relationships and true long-term happiness.

DANGER THIN ICE

Because of concupiscence we are often tempted to ignore warning signs and go against what we know is good for us.

Life Savers

Scripture Signpost

This is the will of God, your holiness: that you refrain from immorality. For God did not call us to impurity but to holiness.

(1 Thessalonians 4:3, 7)

All that God created is good, and not even sin can change that. You have within you the gift of free will, which puts you in charge of your life and helps you develop your good qualities. You have the power to avoid temptation, to say no to it, and to rebound if you give in to it.

We all have sexual feelings. They are part of the wonderful array of feelings God has given us. Those feelings can tempt us to actions which may be inappropriate or wrong, depending on one's vocation. But we are in charge of our bodies and our feelings, and we can avoid sin by rejecting what is wrong and doing what we know is right.

You can find encouragement to do what is right through relationships with adults and friends your own age who help you understand yourself and encourage you to be your best. Avoid those who pressure you to do things you know aren't right.

Good times with friends your own age are an important part of growing in love.

Teachers or mentors can encourage us to develop our interests and talents.

Stay connected to your faith—think about it, pray about it, and ask questions. Look up to adults who show respect for others and love of God. Let God's grace work within you by celebrating the sacraments and by praying daily.

When you make choices that help you overcome temptation and avoid sin, your self-respect grows. You show yourself and others what you are capable of becoming.

True friends encourage one another to make good choices.

Stepping Stones

Being Accountable

A pebble tossed in a river causes several ripples; one domino, when pushed over, can make a whole row fall. Life is the same. A choice you make can have many consequences. You show that you're growing up when you accept the responsibility for the results of your decisions. Here are some ways to do that:

- **Understand that you can influence other people.**

- **Think about the decision you're considering and imagine its possible consequences: "If I do this, then that may happen, and that, and that . . ."**

- **Ask yourself: "Who will be affected by my choice? Will it hurt them? Help them?"**

- **When you make a bad choice, admit your mistake and accept the blame. Is there something you can do to make things better? Use what you learn to help you make a better choice next time.**

- **Realize that you are personally responsible for your choices. Even if no one else knows what you did, it still affects you and your relationship with God.**

Consider the Risks

Answer these questions for the risk named in each link of the chain: Why is this a risk? How can this risk be handled? What's a positive outcome if you don't take this risk?

Not doing homework

_____

_____

_____

Lying to your parents

_____

_____

_____

_____

Watching an R-rated video or movie

_____

_____

_____

Smoking

_____

_____

_____

_____

HomeLink | For Your Family

We shared this chapter. _____

We have these questions or comments:

_____

_____

_____

Come, Holy Spirit,
and shine your light on us!
Come, giver of God's gifts!
Open our hearts to God's love.

Open our lives to God's grace.

(based on the Sequence, or song of praise, from the Mass of Pentecost)

Chapter 6

God our Father, we thank you for always being with us. Jesus, help us bring your presence to others. Holy Spirit, be a source of strength to those experiencing births and deaths. Amen.

Celebrating Life

From conception and birth to aging and death, God is present in our lives. This makes our whole lives a reason to celebrate!

Around the world people celebrate births in various ways. Navajos and Nigerians greet their newborns with songs, Israelis and Swiss commemorate births with newly planted trees, and Tibetans and Vietnamese honor babies with special naming ceremonies.

As Catholics we believe that new life is a gift from God that begins at conception. Whether there is one cell or one billion, they are all human cells. The unborn human person is to be treated with care and respect throughout the mother's **pregnancy.**

God created the mother's uterus to protect and nourish the new life within her. A technical term for the unborn baby who is developing during the first eight weeks is **embryo.** During this very young stage, the baby develops all its body parts. From the third month on, the unborn baby is called a **fetus.** At this time the body systems and organs are all in place, getting bigger and stronger so that the baby can one day survive outside the uterus.

Some families celebrate a birth or adoption by sending a formal announcement to relatives and friends.

At around nine months of development, a baby may weigh seven or eight pounds and is often around twenty-one inches long. The baby is then ready to leave its protective surroundings and enter a much larger world through the process of **childbirth.** At all these stages parents have a responsibility to care for and protect this new life.

For Christians the time of welcoming a child—through biological birth, adoption, or foster parenting—is a wonderful event. Parents see the love they share become an expression of God's creative love.

Even a young child can share in the excitement of expecting a new life.

Scripture
Signpost

You formed my inmost being; you knit me in my mother's womb.

(Psalm 139:13)

God Is with Us

The Church, in all of its diversity, is a communion with God and a unity among people.

(See Catechism, #775.)

While we are all unique individuals, as humans we have much in common. We are part of one human family. We all experience birth and death, and everyone has good times and bad times along the way. Our experiences differ, but we all know what it's like to be happy, fearful, lonely, sad, or angry.

God is with us throughout our lives. Our experiences and the good that other people do help us know God and respond to his love. Being in the human family means noticing when others need God's love and reaching out to help them experience that love through us.

When we meet people, we often know very little about what their lives are like. They may be dealing with personal health problems or family problems. We can assume that everyone we meet needs to be treated with compassion.

Individual pain differs, but all of us have known some kind of hurt and can relate to those who suffer. We can help them know God's healing grace through our comfort and prayer.

As Christians we know that, no matter what happens, we are not alone. God is with those who have just had car accidents, those whose roofs have been blown off by tornadoes, and those who are coping with learning disabilities. God is with the parents who have just been told that the babies they're expecting have serious birth defects.

Those who are hurting remind us of our own challenging times in life and may make us feel uncomfortable. It may be tempting to ignore them or laugh at them. Instead, we can help them know God by the way we share his love with them.

Life-Giving Love

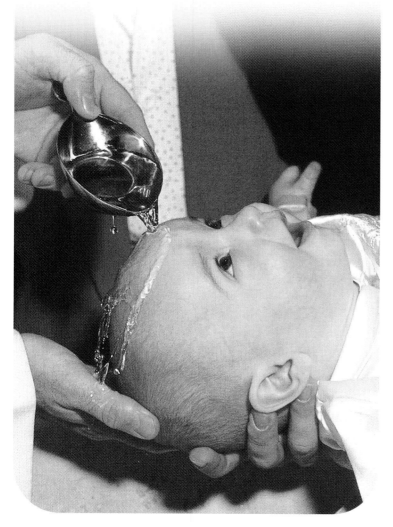

People have a need to mark and celebrate major events and stages in their lives. Some of these events, such as birthdays or anniversaries, are celebrated every year. Others, such as a promotion or a graduation, are celebrated occasionally, at certain moments in time. What events does your family mark on the calendar? What are you celebrating or planning to celebrate?

The Bible describes the people of God as the Body of Christ. "If one part suffers, all the parts suffer with it; if one part is honored, all the parts share its joy" *(1 Corinthians 12:26).* The Church community comes together to honor the mysteries of birth, commitment, suffering, and death. We mark these times with celebration or shared grief. We recognize the presence of God in every stage of life.

At Baptism God the Father and Son are present; through the power of the Spirit, any sins of the baptized are washed away. We gather to celebrate the new life given by God and to welcome the new member of the Church with our prayers.

Through the Sacrament of Holy Orders, a man is consecrated and given a sacred power from Christ through the Church. In Matrimony God's grace is given to the couple to strengthen their love and unity. Life commitments such as these and the public vows of men and women religious are made in community, since they positively affect the whole community of faith. The public witness of those involved is a sign to all of God's ever-present love and faithfulness.

The Church supports the struggles of people who are weakened with age or are seriously ill and reminds them that they are never alone. The Sacrament of **Anointing of the Sick** brings them Christ's healing grace. Through the priest's gentle laying on of hands and anointing with holy oil, Christ blesses the person with strength, courage, and peace. God is present in the compassion we offer those who suffer. We gather to respond to the word of God, pray, and give them our support.

The Church helps those who are dying prepare for their new life in heaven. After someone dies, a Mass of Christian Burial or other **funeral** service is held to celebrate the person's life. We pray for eternal life with God for the one who has died, and we offer comfort to the family. Friends may accompany the family and the body, or the ashes from **cremation,** to the gravesite for **burial.**

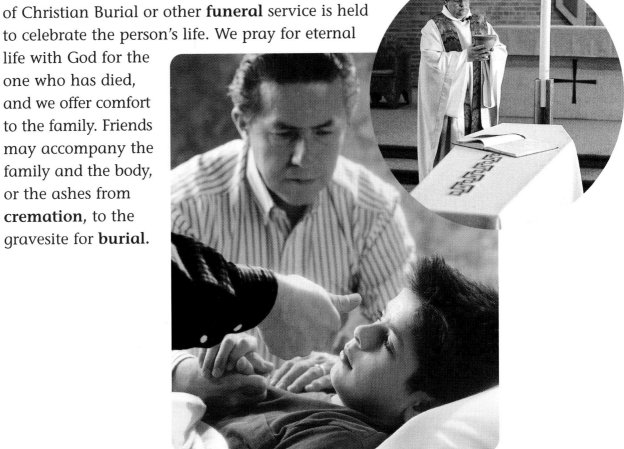

Picture God

In the space below, draw a picture or glue a photo that represents a sad or painful time when you felt God's presence. Use the lines provided to describe what you saw or felt that helped you know God was with you. How can this experience give you more compassion for others?

HomeLink For Your Family

We shared this chapter. _____
We have these questions or comments:

_____

_____

_____

God of compassion,
you take every family under your care.
You know our physical and spiritual needs.
Transform our weakness
by the strength of your grace,
and confirm us in your covenant
so that we may grow in strength and love.

(based on the Opening Prayer B from the Rite of Anointing)

Chapter 7

God our Father, we want to share your love with others. Jesus, God's Son, open our eyes to those who need us. Holy Spirit, lead us to loving and just actions. Amen.

Love in Action

Blessed are the meek, for they will inherit the land.

God made us to have true happiness, which is a state of **beatitude**, or blessedness. Jesus' Beatitudes tell the kind of living it takes to be truly blessed. *(See Matthew 5:3–12.)* The Beatitudes are signs of God's kingdom and a source of hope in difficult times.

Choose to be meek. Living this way calls for the humility to be grateful for the gifts God gives you. Meekness helps you accept those gifts and develop them without using them to harm or humiliate others. Being meek means seeing kindness as a strength, not a weakness. It means being gentle with people and things and not being pushy or violent in order to get your own way.

Blessed are they who hunger and thirst for righteousness, for they will be satisfied.

Choose to be just. You know how it feels to crave a favorite food. Jesus calls us to hunger and thirst for the just treatment of others. Be aware of the way people around you are mistreated or discriminated against, and do something about it in the best way you can. Be ready to stand up for what is right and good and, if necessary, to accept ridicule for your position. When you're wrong, admit it; accept the consequences of your choices. Be true to yourself and your good values.

Blessed are the clean of heart, for they will see God.

Choose to be clean of heart. Having a clean heart means developing an honest, healthy view of yourself and others. Respect yourself and others and the gift of sexuality. Practice moderation in what you eat and how you dress. Don't give in to negative pressure to use drugs or alcohol or to become sexually active. Closely evaluate the messages you receive through the media.

Blessed are the peacemakers, for they will be called children of God.

Choose to make peace. Being a peacemaker means showing mercy and kindness to those who are weaker than you in body, mind, or spirit. Don't take advantage of them. Forgive those who hurt you, and listen to those who disagree with you. Be willing to make peace through discussion and compromise, even though it may seem to take longer than a fight. Make peace within yourself by valuing who you are.

When we follow the Beatitudes, we help prepare the way for the fullness of God's kingdom.

God's Messengers

People have often searched the heavens for signs of changing weather. In recent years satellites and other technological developments have made the important job of weather forecasting a more accurate science. For their own safety people are forewarned about blizzards, flash floods, tornadoes, and hurricanes. But when the weather isn't pleasant, the weather forecaster is often blamed.

Every Christian has a role similar to that of a weather forecaster. That role is being a prophet. Our job is to be alert to all that may be morally harmful. When we see signs of danger, it's up to us to warn others. However, being a prophet is usually not popular or easy because not everyone wants to hear the truth.

In the Bible prophets were considered messengers of God. Along with warning people to leave their wicked ways and turn back to God, they gave messages of hope based on God's promises. You may be familiar with contemporary prophets, such as Cesar Chavez, who spoke out for the rights of migrant workers.

Catholics Believe

True happiness is found in doing God's will.

(See Catechism, #1723.)

We're all called to be God's messengers. How do you respond to this call?

God's **prophetic** messengers say that greed is wrong. They say the good that people do is more important than the things they own. They challenge people to care for each person as a sister or brother. Prophets say that trying to get away with something because "everybody does it" makes the world a less trusting place. They say there's too much emphasis on sex and not enough on sexuality and chastity. They challenge people to stop blaming others for their own mistakes.

Not everyone who warns against the dangers of sin is a prophet. Anyone who claims to speak for God but leads people into destructive behavior is a false prophet. In addition, even a true prophet can be mistaken about a particular matter.

As a Christian you are called to be prophetic. If you see each person as a child of God and care about others enough to want to keep them from doing wrong, then you'll find ways to say and do whatever is needed. You can speak up for what is right and just. You can look for peaceful solutions to problems and be a sign of hope to those around you.

Oscar Romero and Katharine Drexel were effective messengers of God who worked for the good of others.

Signs of God's Kingdom

Images help people understand ideas. The image of a kingdom is often used to represent a carefree, happy place for a privileged few. The Church uses the image of a kingdom to describe a place of relationship with God, a place of happiness, where God's justice rules.

Jesus proclaimed God's kingdom on earth. Our relationship with God is still developing and will come to fullness one day when our growing in love is complete. As members of the Church, and through our positive and loving relationships, we are signs of God's kingdom on earth. By sharing God's love in our world, we quicken the time when the kingdom will be fulfilled.

We are signs of God's kingdom when we work for justice and peace in all our relationships.

We show our solidarity when we act together to create a just, caring world.

Christian Living

Here are some practical and simple ways you can be a sign of God's kingdom.

- **Think about your abilities, and see how you can use them to help others.**

- **Look for volunteer opportunities at home, at school, or in your parish or neighborhood.**

- **Visit someone who needs company, or call, e-mail, or write a note.**

- **Talk to someone you usually ignore.**

- **Spend time with a young child.**

- **Give help without expecting anything in return.**

In the fullness of God's kingdom, prophets will no longer be needed because sin and evil won't exist. As members of the Church community, we pave the way for that kingdom when we live in ways that promote justice and peace.

Seeing each person as a child of God moves us to share others' sufferings and work for the good of all. Many individuals with similar goals and many Churches form local, national, and international groups that work for justice. When we work in **solidarity**, with belief and trust in God, we know that anything is possible. God's kingdom may be realized.

As individuals and as a Church, we contribute to the growth of the kingdom. We look within ourselves to see how we are moving toward blessedness. We ask, "What do I do every day that makes me a better person? Is my life based on God's justice? How can I live God's peace today? How can I share God's love?" And how do we as a Christian community answer these questions?

My Pledge

Sharing God's love requires a real commitment. Take some time to think about the best ways you can live the Beatitudes. Write specific ideas on the plaque below.

I promise to live the Beatitudes.

I will show meekness by _____.

I will work for justice at _____ by

_____.

I will be clean of heart by _____.

I will be a peacemaker by _____.

Signed,

_____

HomeLink For Your Family

We shared this chapter. _____

We have these questions or comments:

_____

_____

_____

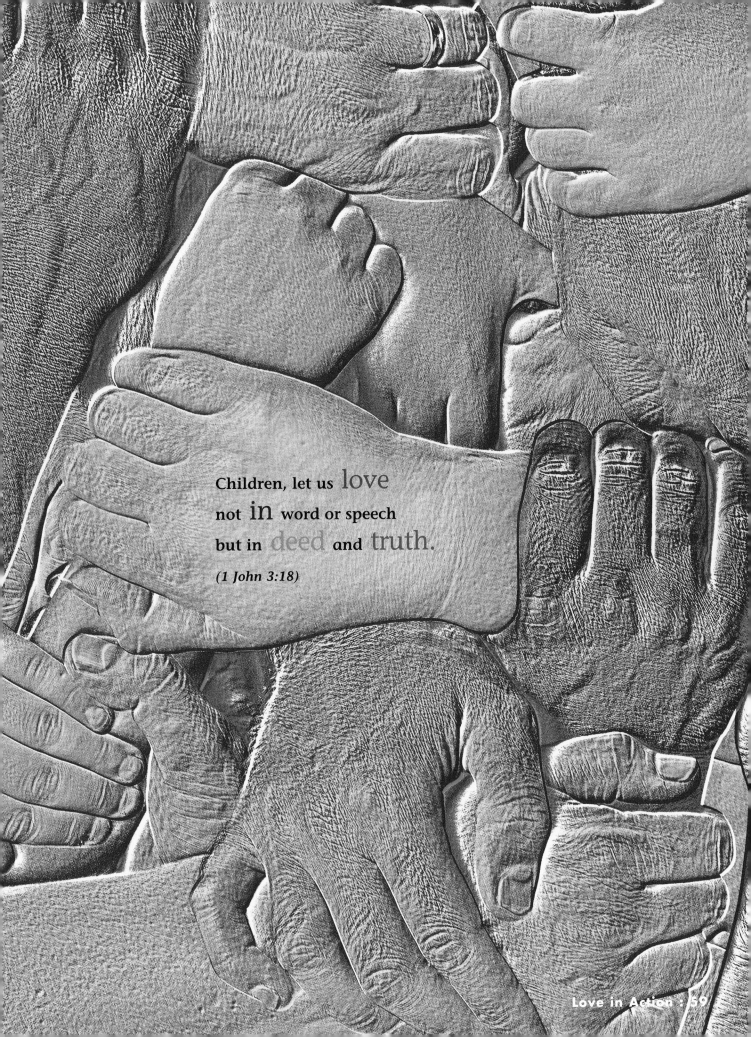

Children, let us love
not in word or speech
but in deed and truth.

(1 John 3:18)

Prayers and Resources

The Sign of the Cross In the name of the Father,
and of the Son,
and of the Holy Spirit.
Amen.

The Lord's Prayer Our Father, who art in heaven,
hallowed be thy name;
thy kingdom come;
thy will be done on earth as it is in heaven.
Give us this day our daily bread;
and forgive us our trespasses
as we forgive those who trespass against us;
and lead us not into temptation.
but deliver us from evil.
Amen.

Hail Mary Hail, Mary, full of grace,
the Lord is with you!
Blessed are you among women,
and blessed is the fruit of your womb, Jesus.
Holy Mary, Mother of God,
pray for us sinners,
now and at the hour of our death.
Amen.

Glory to the Father (Doxology)

Glory to the Father, and to the Son, and to the
  Holy Spirit:
as it was in the beginning, is now, and will be
  for ever.
Amen.

Blessing Before Meals

Bless us, O Lord, and these your gifts
which we are about to receive from your goodness.
Through Christ our Lord.
Amen.

Thanksgiving After Meals

We give you thanks for all your gifts, almighty God,
living and reigning now and for ever.
Amen.

A Family Prayer

Lord our God, bless this household.
May we be blessed with health, goodness of heart,
gentleness, and the keeping of your law.
We give thanks to you,
Father, Son, and Holy Spirit,
now and for ever.
Amen.

The Great Commandment

"You shall love the Lord, your God, with all your
heart, with all your being, with all your strength,
and with all your mind, and your neighbor as
yourself."
(Luke 10:27)

Prayer to the Holy Spirit

Come, Holy Spirit, fill the hearts of your faithful.
And kindle in them the fire of your love.
Send forth your Spirit and they shall be created.
And you will renew the face of the earth.
Lord,
by the light of your Holy Spirit
you have taught the hearts of your faithful.
In that same Spirit
help us choose what is right
and always rejoice in your consolation.
We ask this through Christ our Lord.
Amen.

Act of Contrition

My God,
I am sorry for my sins with all my heart.
In choosing to do wrong
and failing to do good,
I have sinned against you
whom I should love above all things.
I firmly intend, with your help,
to do penance,
to sin no more,
and to avoid whatever leads me to sin.
Our Savior Jesus Christ
suffered and died for us.
In his name, my God, have mercy.

The Jesus Prayer

Lord Jesus Christ,
Son of God,
have mercy on me, a sinner.
Amen.

The Beatitudes

Blessed are the poor in spirit,
for theirs is the kingdom of heaven.
Blessed are they who mourn,
for they will be comforted.
Blessed are the meek,
for they will inherit the land.
Blessed are they who hunger and thirst for
righteousness,
for they will be satisfied.
Blessed are the merciful,
for they will be shown mercy.
Blessed are the clean of heart,
for they will see God.
Blessed are the peacemakers,
for they will be called children of God.
Blessed are they who are persecuted for the sake
of righteousness,
for theirs is the kingdom of heaven.
(Matthew 5:3–10)

The Ten Commandments

1. I am the Lord your God. You shall not have strange gods before me.
2. You shall not take the name of the Lord your God in vain.
3. Remember to keep holy the Lord's day.
4. Honor your father and your mother.
5. You shall not kill.
6. You shall not commit adultery.
7. You shall not steal.
8. You shall not bear false witness against your neighbor.
9. You shall not covet your neighbor's wife.
10. You shall not covet your neighbor's goods.

Works of Mercy

Corporal (for the body)	Spiritual (for the spirit)
Feed the hungry.	Warn the sinner.
Give drink to the thirsty.	Teach the ignorant.
Clothe the naked.	Counsel the doubtful.
Shelter the homeless.	Comfort the sorrowful.
Visit the sick.	Bear wrongs patiently.
Visit the imprisoned.	Forgive injuries.
Bury the dead.	Pray for the living and the dead.

Gifts of the Holy Spirit

Wisdom
Understanding
Right judgment (Counsel)
Courage (Fortitude)
Knowledge
Reverence (Piety)
Wonder and awe (Fear of the Lord)

Fruits of the Spirit

Charity	Generosity
Joy	Gentleness
Peace	Faithfulness
Patience	Modesty
Kindness	Self-control
Goodness	Chastity

Virtues

Theological	Cardinal
Faith	Prudence
Hope	Justice
Love	Fortitude
	Temperance